The World War in

Prophecy

*The Downfall of the Kaiser and
The End of the Dispensation*

by

Henry Clay Morrison

*First Fruits Press
Wilmore, Kentucky
c2015*

The World War in Prophecy: The Downfall of the Kaiser and The End of the Dispensation by H. C. Morrison

First Fruits Press, © 2015
Previously published by the Pentecostal Publishing Company, ©1917

Digital version at
http://place.asburyseminary.edu/firstfruitsheritagematerial/28/

ISBN: 9781621711407 (Print), 9781621711391 (Digital)

Morrison, H. C. (Henry Clay), 1857-1942.
 The world war in prophecy : the downfall of the Kaiser and the end of the dispensation / by H.C. Morrison.
 Fifth edition
 128 pages ; 21 cm.
 Wilmore, Ky. : First Fruits Press, c2015.
 Reprint. Previously published: Louisville, KY : Pentecostal Publishing Company, ©1917.
 ISBN: 9781621711407 (pbk.)
 1. World War, 1914-1918 -- Prophecies. I. Title.
D524 .M6 2015   220.1

Cover design by Haley Hill

First Fruits Press
The Academic Open Press of Asbury Theological Seminary
204 N. Lexington Ave., Wilmore, KY 40390
859-858-2236
first.fruits@asburyseminary.edu
asbury.to/firstfruits

The World War in Prophecy

The Downfall of the Kaiser

and

The End of the Dispensation

BY

Rev. H. C. MORRISON, D. D.

Author of "World Tour of Evangelism," "Life Sketches
and Sermons," The "Second Coming," "Romanism
and Ruin," "The Two Lawyers" "Thoughts for
the Thoughtful," "The Confession of a
Backslider," "Prophecies Fulfilled
and Fulfilling," Etc.

Thirteenth Thousand.

PENTECOSTAL PUBLISHING COMPANY
LOUISVILLE, KENTUCKY

DEDICATION.

This book is affectionately dedicated to Mrs. Mary A. Crawford, of Madison, Georgia, whose helpful sympathy and prayers have followed me through many years of arduous toil, and whose liberality has proven a great blessing to Asbury College.

TABLE OF CONTENTS.

"In the beginning God created the heaven and the earth." Gen. 1:1.

"The heavens declare the glory of God; the firmament sheweth his handiwork. Day unto day uttereth speech, and night unto night sheweth knowledge." Psa. 19:1, 2.

"Declaring the end from the beginning, and from ancient times the things that are not yet done, saying, My counsel shall stand, and I will do all my pleasure." Isa. 46:10.

CHAPTER I.

A FEW GREAT FACTS.

We desire, in the beginning of the discussions to follow, to call attention to a few great facts, the first of which is, that this universe did not come into existence by accident, and is not governed by chance. God created all things, and placed the whole under law, and His supreme will reigns over all.

HE HAS A DEFINITE PROGRAM for the direction and control of all affairs upon this planet. He cannot be hurried, and He cannot be retarded or diverted from *His Program*. Nothing is done by chance in the administration of His Kingdom, but all things move with beautiful order and harmony, and the great events of history come to pass at their appointed time.

Few subjects of study can be more entertaining and profitable to the devout mind, than to search the Scriptures in order to find out just where we are in the Divine program of the history of our world. The second fact, to which we call attention is this: GOD HAS BROKEN TIME UP INTO AGES, OR DISPENSATIONS. Each dispensation closes with the judgments of God upon the wicked; the sifting out of the wheat from the chaff; and, each dispensation prepares the way for a larger revelation, and a better age. The first dispensation closed with the Flood. After ample warning and opportunity for repentance, God swept away the rebellious multitudes, sparing only eight righteous souls, Noah and his family. For a long time the memory of the Flood, with its fearful lesson, the fact that God would send His judgments upon the wicked, had a salutary effect upon the race, and prepared the way for the calling of Abraham, and the inauguration of the Hebrew dispensation.

The Hebrew dispensation was a time of great revelation and blessing; the knowledge of God was largely spread through the earth. In the development of the race, the understanding of the Divine character, and the Divine government, it far surpassed the antediluvian age. The chosen people, the Israelites, however, were prone to backsliding, and reached the climax of wickedness in the crucifixion of our Lord Jesus Christ.

John the Baptist pointed to the coming end of this dispensation when he declared, "The axe is laid unto the root of the trees." The tree of the Hebrew dispensation was hewn down when the Roman army captured Jerusalem and carried her people into captivity from which they have not been restored.

When our Lord Jesus on the cross exclaimed, "It is finished," He not only meant that in the giving up of His life the great work of the atonement was finished, but the age—a dispensation—had come to its closing chapter; a new and higher order of things was to be introduced into the world. The Christian Church was to be organized, and the Gospel dispensation ushered in, which in contrast with any other dispensation of the past, was far to outshine them all.

The world of mankind has made far more progress in everything that goes to contribute to human happiness, during the Gospel dispensation, than during all the ages of the past. Under the enlightenment of the Gospel, general civilization has spread among the nations of the earth. Almost all the inhabitants of the world have felt, to some extent, the benefits of the gracious influence of the Gospel age. The great discoveries of nature's resources and the adaptation of those resources to the needs of men, with the innumerable inventions that have helped forward human progress, have come to us through the quickening and enlightenment of the human intellect through the gracious influence of the Gospel. Truly Christ's coming has not only brought life, but it has brought us life more abundant. It is safe to say that the light of the present dispensation, as contrasted with any past age, is as the Morning Star in its beauty, compared to the glow-worm in the swamp.

The Christian reader will remember that in the Divine program there is to come another dispensation, which will surpass the present as far as the Gospel dispensation surpasses the Hebrew age. As the Hebrew prepared the way for this, this is preparing the way for the golden age foretold in prophecy, in which the Lord Jesus Christ Himself shall reign supreme; when men shall learn war no more, when swords are beaten into plowshares, and spears into pruning-hooks; when peace and fraternity shall pervade the entire earth; when the kingdoms of this world shall become the kingdoms of our Lord and His Christ; when the knowledge of the glory of the Lord shall cover the earth as the waters cover the sea.

The third fact to which we call attention is this: In revealing Himself, His laws, His will, and His love for the human race, God has chosen largely the PROPHETIC METHOD. He has spoken to holy men, and sent them to declare His will and testimony to His people. By means of this method God has given us a revelation capable of positive proof, placing the Bible entirely beyond the possibility of guesswork or forgery, on the high and solid foundation of absolute trustworthiness. The prophetic method enables us to prove by the well-known facts of history, that the holy Seers of old were inspired by the Holy Ghost to speak and to write.

"For prophecy came not of old time by the will of man: but holy men of God spake as *they were moved* by the Holy Ghost." 2 Pet. 1:21.

"And the Lord hath sent unto you all his servants the Prophets, rising early and sending them; but ye have not hearkened, nor inclined your ear to hear." Jer. 25:4.

CHAPTER II.

THE PROPHETIC METHOD OF REVELATION.

We have every reason to believe that the God who created the universe, Who built this world and placed upon it intelligent, moral beings, will reveal Himself to these beings. It is in harmoy with the eternal fitness of things that we should find among men just such a book as the Bible—a revelation from God. And it is eminently proper and to be desired, that the Bible be of such a character that its Divine origin is self-evident; that it contain in and of itself, positive proof of its inspiration.

We do not propose any general discussion of the various evidences of the genuineness of Christianity, and the proofs of the Divine origin of the Holy Scriptures, but we do wish to impress upon our readers the fact that one of the clearest and

(15)

most satisfactory evidences of the inspiration of the Bible is found in the prophecies contained in the Scriptures, and their very remarkable and minute fulfillment.

It was the wisdom of God to give us the Holy Scriptures in two books; or, to be more accurate, in the collection of a number of books in two volumes—the Old and the New Testament. The Old Testament was written long before the New. The Old Testament is fully endorsed, and liberally quoted by our Lord Jesus and His Apostles, who were the authors of the New Testament. The Old Testament is largely made up of prophecies; the New Testament is largely a record of the fulfillment of those prophecies. An American scholar has wisely said, "The New Testament is shut up in the Old, and the Old Testament is opened up in the New."

These two collections of books splendidly confirm the truthfulness and reliability of each other. As might be supposed, God proposed to give a living revelation of Himself of such character that its truthfulness could be proven beyond all possibility of cavil or doubt. It was His wisdom to take into His counsels holy men of old to whom He revealed the secrets of the ages, and while they taught the people of their time their obligations to God and their fellow-beings, the blessings to be secured by obedient and virtuous living, and the disaster which would inevitably befall the wicked and rebellious, they also looked far into the future and predicted the coming events of human history with such accuracy and detail that the Scriptures are lifted entirely out of the realm of uncertainty, or the possibility of human forgery, on to the high plain of absolute and positive proof of their Divine origin and inspiration.

The great pivotal events of the history of the world are so faithfully foretold and so accurately described by the ancient prophets, that there is but one possible way to account for their knowledge of coming events, and that is, they were inspired by the Holy Spirit.

Before the Israelites entered the land of Canaan, Moses prophesied their apostasy and final dispersion among their heathen captors. The fall of Babylon was faithfully predicted by a holy prophet when the city in its riches, splendor and strength looked as if it could withstand every foe, and wear out the ages. Prophet after prophet foretold the fall of Jerusalem when their warnings were sneered at by an arrogant and rebellious people, who were hurrying forward to their doom, so faithfully portrayed by the prophets of the Lord.

Seven hundred years before the angelic choir startled the Shepherds as they watched their flocks an Judean hills, the Prophet Micah had pointed out the country, and named the village, where the

Lord Jesus should be born, when he wrote: "But thou Bethlehem Ephratah, though thou be little among the thousands of Judah, yet out of thee shall he come forth unto me that is to be ruler in Israel." Centuries afterward, when the Wise Men, following the star, came to Jerusalem, inquiring where Christ should be born, asserting that they had seen His star in the East and had come to worship Him, Herod the king, was greatly troubled, and all Jerusalem with him, and he demanded of the chief priests and scribes where Jesus should be born; they answered him: "In Bethlehem of Judea: for thus it is written by the prophet." They referred him to the same prophecy of Micah, quoted above.

It is interesting to note the fact that the prophets go into very minute details in some of their descriptions of future events, so that there is absolutely no accounting for their knowledge of these details except on the basis of their Divine inspiration. Many hundreds of years before our Lord made His triumphal entry into Jerusalem, we find the prophet Zechariah proclaiming, "Rejoice greatly, O daughter of Zion; shout, O daughter of Jerusalem; behold, thy King cometh unto thee: He is just, and having salvation; lowly, and riding upon an ass, and upon a colt the foal of an ass." Turning to Matthew's Gospel, 21st chapter, we find this prophecy was fulfilled in every detail.

No one of the ancient prophets had a clearer insight into the person and mission of our Lord Jesus, than Isaiah. So clear is his vision, and so minute and accurate are his descriptions, that hundreds of years before the birth of the Savior he puts down incidents which occurred in His life as if they had already taken place. He describes His humble person; he tells of His patient and silent sufferings: "He is brought as a lamb to the slaughter, and as a sheep before her shearers is dumb, so

He opened not His mouth. He was bruised
for our iniquities: the chastisement of our
peace was upon Him; and with His stripes
we are healed. He made his grave with
the wicked, and with the rich in His
death." Then the prophet's horizon is
lifted and he beholds the gracious outcome
and results of the sufferings of our Lord,
and exclaims in triumph, "He shall see of
the travail of His soul, and shall be satisfied." This 53rd chapter of Isaiah's
prophecy is so perfectly fulfilled in the history of Christ's sufferings, as we find them
recorded in the Gospel, that the Christian
may rejoice in the absolute certainty of
the Divine inspiration of the holy prophet.

King David was not only the Psalm
writer for Israel, but he was also a prophet, and is constantly referring in the
Psalms to our Lord Jesus. Among other
things, he describes an incident which occurred at the foot of the Cross on the day
of the crucifixion. The Psalmist says,

"They part My garments among them, and cast lots upon My vesture." This was written many hundred years before the tragic event on Calvary. But Matthew, in the 27th chapter and 35th verse, shows how accurately this prophecy of the Psalmist was fulfilled: "They parted My garments among them, and upon My vesture did they cast lots."

We cannot understand how any intelligent, fairminded being, reading this ancient prophecy and its remarkable fulfillment, will be able to question the Divine inspiration of the Psalmist David. Again, David says, speaking of Christ, "He keepeth all His bones: not one of them is broken." In John, 19th chapter, it reads: "Then came the soldiers, and brake the legs of the first, and of the other which was crucified with him. But when they came to Jesus, and saw that He was dead already, they brake not His legs. For these things were done, that the Scripture should be fulfilled, A bone of Him shall not be broken."

It will be remembered that the soldier did, in order to ascertain whether our Lord was actually dead, pierce His side with a spear, while his companions stood gazing on to see if the spear would bring forth any manifestation of life. This was in fulfillment of a prophecy in Zechariah 12: 10: "And they shall look upon Me whom they have pierced."

We might give enough prophecies with their fulfillment to fill a large volume, but what we have given is amply sufficient to prove the trustworthiness of the prophecies contained in the Holy Scriptures.

"And he changeth the times and the seasons: he removeth kings, and setteth up kings; he giveth wisdom unto the wise, and knowledge to them that know understanding. He revealeth the deep and secret things: He knoweth what is in the darkness, and the light dwelleth with him." Dan. 2:21, 22.

CHAPTER III.

NEBUCHADNEZZAR'S IMAGE.

While much of prophecy clusters about the world's Redeemer, predicting His coming, His teaching, His sufferings and death, His resurrection and triumph, it must be understood that the prophets also foretold many things concerning world history, and the great events which are to occur as the Divine program goes forward to the final exaltation and glory, when He shall be crowned King of kings, and Lord of lords.

One of these prophecies which is of special interest at the present time, is to be found in the second chapter of the book of Daniel. Nebuchadnezzar, king of Babylon, in a dream saw a great image. Its head was of gold, its breasts and arms were of silver, its belly and thighs were of brass, its legs of iron, and its feet part of

iron and part of clay.   The King also saw
in his vision that a stone was cut,
without hands, which smote the image
upon his feet, and broke in pieces the entire image, until it became like the chaff
of the summer threshing floors; and the
wind carried it away; but the stone which
smote the image, became a great mountain,
and filled the whole earth.

The reader who is acquainted with the
book of Daniel will recall that Nebuchadnezzar had the dream but entirely forgot
details.   Being troubled to know its mean-
ing, he called for his astrologers and wise
men, and demanded that they should tell
him the dream and its interpretation.   The
wise men insisted that he should tell the
dream, and they would give the interpretation.   At this he became angry and declared that all the wise men of Babylon
should be slain.   When Daniel was sought
by the executioner he asked for time, and
went to God in prayer Who gave him both

the dream, and its interpretation, which Daniel explained to the full satisfaction of the king. The very fact that Daniel gave to the king his own dream, in all its details, convinced the king that its interpretation was fully trustworthy.

Daniel's interpretation of the dream revealed the fact that there were to be four great world empires, of which Nebuchadnezzar, representing the head of gold, was the first, reigning over the Babylonian empire. The second empire represented by the breast of silver, was the Medo-Persian, which was soon to follow. And the third, represented by the belly and thighs of brass, was the Grecian empire which overthrew the Medo-Persian. The fourth world empire which overthrew the Grecian, was the Roman, which was represented by the legs of iron, and is described as being exceedingly fierce and destructive.

These prophecies of Daniel, describing the image to Nebuchadnezzar, have been remarkably fulfilled. Had the Roman empire been followed by another great world empire, Daniel's prophecy would have broken down, and history would have proven him inaccurate; but fortunately for the Bible, the Word of God, which never makes mistakes, and cannot fail, true to Daniel's description of the image, at the fall of the Roman empire, many smaller kingdoms, representing the toes of this image, were set up, and have existed ever since the breaking up of the Roman empire.

We are now in that period of history represented by the toes of the image; and the reader will remember that these toes were part of iron, and part of clay, representing the strength and weakness of the kingdom of the world today. Any one who knows anything of world conditions is well aware of the fact that there is a state of division and strife among the peoples of all nations at the present time. The great war now in progress has had quite a tendency to unite the people of the various nations for self-protection.

It is claimed by some, and not without sound argument, that Germany hurried up this war in order to save her own nation from an internal revolution brought on by the rapid growth of radical socialism. Those acquainted with current history, are well aware of the fact that there have recently been great internal disturbances in Spain, and Alfonzo has been trembling on his throne. Mexico has been a slaughter pen of internal strife, Greece has been rent asunder, Ireland was on the verge of open rebellion and war against England when the great war broke out. Social disturbance and conflict between labor and capital, have menaced the peace and prosperity of these United States for years. Since the Russo-Japanese war Russia's internal conditions have been like a smoking volcano, trembling with the constant threat of fearful eruption.

World conditions immediately before our great war are accurately described by the iron and clay—the strength and weakness —foretold in the toes of the great image. We do not see how any one who believes the Bible to be an inspired book, can consistently reject the prophecies of Daniel; and we do not see how any one who believes Daniel's prophecy can reasonably evade the fact that we are in the very "toe age" of the great image; and this brings us face to face with the glorious fact that we are rapidly approaching the time when the stone, which is the Kingdom of Christ, is to break in pieces, and consume all these kingdoms, and fill the whole earth.

Daniel, describing this period of the division of the great Roman empire into many smaller kingdoms, and the mixed and weakened condition of these kingdoms, says, "And in the days of these kings shall the God of heaven set up a kingdom, which shall never be destroyed: and the kingdom shall not be left to other people, but it shall break in pieces and consume all these kingdoms, and it shall stand forever."

It is an interesting fact, and well worth the serious consideration of thinking people, everywhere, that just at this. time, when the prophetic finger points to the closing of a dispensation, that the great war should have broken out, involving practically, all nations in a destructive strife without parallel in the history of the world. It looks as if the breaking up of the kingdoms was at least in its beginnings. A number of kings are at the present time in exile, and it is the very general prophecy of thoughtful statesmen that some of the world's greatest empires will go to pieces, and some of the most powerful thrones will be vacated and destroyed at the close of the war.

There is one thing absolutely certain: if Daniel's prophecies are trustworthy, we are rapidly approaching the end of this dispensation, and the inauguration of a far better one. Daniel's prophecies are trustworthy because his interpretation of the different parts of the image has been literally fulfilled, and is plainly written in the pages of secular history. The four great kingdoms have arisen, flourished, and fallen. The territory once occupied by these vast empires is now occupied by a number of smaller kingdoms, and these kingdoms, partly strong and partly broken, are before our eyes today in actual current history. Daniel's prophecies, in their remarkable fulfillment up to the present time, prove him trustworthy.

Shall we not lift up our heads with hope, that the coming of our Lord draweth near!

"How art thou fallen from heaven, O Lucifer, son of the morning! how art thou cut down to the ground, which didst weaken the nations! For thou hast said in thine heart, I will ascend into heaven, I will exalt my throne above the stars of God: I will sit also upon the mount of the congregation, in the sides of the north: I will ascend above the heights of the clouds; I will be like the most High." Isa. 14:12, 13, 14.

CHAPTER IV.

SATAN'S AMBITION TO RULE THE WORLD.

The Scriptures teach us that through ambition to exalt himself to supreme rulership, a great angel became the devil. From the Scriptures we also learn that since his fall he has constantly sought absolute rulership of this planet and its inhabitants, and while he has met with a large degree of success, he has not yet been able to boast himself of complete mastery.

Satan is a great counterfeiter. It seems he has always sought to find out the Divine plan, and as nearly as possible, imitate God's scheme of government, to deceive the people and bring them under his sway.

God determined in the redemption of the race and the restitution of order and happiness in the world, to incarnate Himself in humanity, to blend two natures into one, to give the world a great King Who combined in Himself the humanity which enabled Him to sympathize with men, and the Deity which enabled Him to save men. For many centuries Satan has been seeking to follow something of the same method in world government. His plan has been to bring the whole world under the government of one man, and to bring that man under his control, filling that man with his spirit of merciless cruelty, and thus governing the earth himself through a human agent.

Several times in past history he has made remarkable success in this effort, and will no doubt come more nearly approximating that success in the Man of Sin, frequently referred to in the Scriptures, who is to appear in the closing days of this dispensation. All of the great world rulers in the earlier history of the human race, were not only men of marvelous power, but of desperate wickedness. Alexander the Great was no doubt a

supreme effort of Satan to produce a man
of sin, who should rule the world with des-
potic tyranny, robbing man of the liberty
and happiness planned for him by his
Maker. He was followed by Julius Cæsar
who sought to rule the whole world; and he
was followed by Napoleon Bonaparte, a
marvelous military genius, almost a super-
man, who shook the world with his powerful armies, and who was as merciless
as he was brilliant. The human suffering
which his insatiable ambition entailed upon the race is incalculable. It has been
so with all the monstrous men who, inspired by Satan, have sought world power,
and heedless of the devastation and ruin
which they have spread abroad among
their fellow beings, have used all their
large capacities, no doubt quickened and
increased by the inspiration of Satan himself.

Satan's last effort to date, for world rulership, has headed up in the German

Kaiser. It is not to be supposed that any
of these men who have aspired to world
rulership, understand that their ambition
has been inspired by the devil. They have
doubtless believed themselves to be bene-
factors. By some strange method of rea-
soning they convinced themselves that they
ought to rule; that their undisputed sway
would be best for the race; that they would
be able to introduce a better social order
among men. This is evidently true of the
Kaiser. He does not dream that he is the
agent of the devil; that Satanic influence
dominates his mind, and has nursed and
developed in him a proud and arrogant
ambition through the years to control and
become the military dictator of the world.

While the Kaiser makes loud and fre-
quent religious professions, and believes
himself to be the agent of the God of heav-
en, his spirit and methods demonstrate the
fact that he is the agent of the *god* of this
world. Never in the history of the race,

has any military chieftain shown himself more indifferent to the laws of civilization, more callous and merciless, deaf and indifferent to the cries of suffering humanity than the German Kaiser during the progress of this great world war. We cannot recall a single action that, in the least degree, suggests that he has been for one moment influenced by the Spirit of the Prince of Peace, or governed by the holy God of compassion and mercy.

It will be remembered that directly after His baptism, Jesus was taken to a high mountain by the devil, where He was shown the kingdoms and glory of this world. Satan claimed to own them, and offered them to Christ if He would worship Him; make Satan His god; place Satan first, in world rulership. While the devil was offering a great prize, and no doubt lying, he was careful to reserve for himself the highest place. If he bestowed the gift which he proposed, Christ must worship him.

With the permission of Mr. Louis Sy-
berkrop, of Des Moines, Iowa, we are ad-
ding to this chapter his remarkable piece
of satire purporting to be a letter from Satan to the German Kaiser:

THE INFERNAL REGION.

June 28, 1917.

*To Wilhelm von Hohenzollern, King of
Prussia, Emperor of All Germany and
Envoy Extraordinary of Almighty God.*

My Dear Wilhelm:

I can call you by that familiar name for
I have always been very close to you, much
closer than you could ever know.

From the time that you were yet an un-
developed being in your mother's womb I
have shaped your destiny for my own purpose.

In the days of Rome I created a rough-
neck known in history as Nero; he was a
vulgar character and suited my purpose at
that particular time.   In these modern
days a classic demon and efficient super-
criminal was needed, and as I know the
Hohenzollern blood I picked you as my special instrument to place on earth an annex
of hell; I gave you abnormal ambition, like-
wise an over supply of egotism that you
might not discover your own failings; I

twisted your mind to that of a mad man
with certain normal tendencies to carry
you by, a most dangerous character placed
in power; I gave you the power of a hyp-
notist and a certain magnetic force that
you might sway your people. I am re-
sponsible for the deformed arm that hangs
helpless on your left, for your crippled condition embitters your life and destroys all
noble impulses that might otherwise cause
me anxiety, but your strong sword arm
is driven by your ambition that squelches
all sentiment and pity; I placed in your
soul a deep hatred of all things English,
for of all nations on earth I hate England
most; wherever England plants her flag
she brings order out of chaos and the hated
Cross follows the Union Jack; under her
rule wild tribes become tillers of the soil
and in due time practical citizens; she is
the great civilizer of the globe and I HATE
HER. I planted in your soul a cruel hatred of your mother because SHE was
English, and left my good friend Bismarck
to fan the flame I had kindled. Recent
history proves how well our work was
done. It broke your royal mother's heart
but I gained my purpose.

The inherited disease of the Hohenzol-
lerns killed your father, just as it will kill

you, and you became the ruler of Germany
and a tool of mine sooner than I expected.
To assist you and further hasten my
work I sent you three evil spirits, Nietz-
sche, Treitschke and later Bernhardi,
whose teachings inflamed the youths of
Germany, who in good time would be willing and loyal subjects and eager to spill
their blood and pull your chestnuts, *Yours
and Mine.* The spell has been perfect—you
cast your ambitious eyes toward the Med-
iterranean, Egypt, India and the Dardan-
elles, and you began your great railway
to Bagdad, but the ambitious archduke and
his more ambitious wife, stood in your
way. It was then that I sowed the seed
in your heart that blossomed into the as-
sassination of the Duke and his wife, and
all hell smiled when it saw how cleverly
you saddled the crime on Servia. I saw
you set sail for the Fjords of Norway and
I knew you would prove an alibi. How
cleverly done; so much like your noble
grandfather who also secured an assassin
to remove old King Frederick of Denmark,
and later robbed that country of two prov-
inces that gave Germany an opportunity
'o become a naval power. Murder is dirty
work but it takes a Hohenzollern to make
a way and get by.

Your opportunity was at hand; you set the world on fire and the bells of hell ringing; your rape on Belgium caused much joy; it was the beginning, the foundation of a perfect hell on earth. The destruction of noble cathedrals and other infinite works of art was hailed with joy in the infernal region. You made war on friends and foes alike, the murder of civilians showed my teachings had borne fruit. Your treachery toward neutral nations hastened a universal upheaval, THE THING I MOST DESIRED. Your undersea warfare is a master stroke—from the smallest mackerel boat to the great Lusitania, you show no favorites; as a war lord you stand supreme for you have no mercy; you have no consideration for the baby clinging to its mother's breast as they both go down into the deep together only to be torn apart and leisurely devoured by sharks down among the corals.

I have strolled over the battlefields of Belgium and France. I have seen your hand of destruction everywhere; its all your work, super-fiend that I made you; I have seen the fields of Poland, now a wilderness fit for prowling beasts only; no merry children in Poland now, they all succumbed to frost and starvation. I

drifted down into Galacia where formerly
Jews and Gentiles lived happily together;
I found but ruins and ashes; I felt a curi-
ous pride in my pupil for it was all above
my expectation. I was in Belgium when
you drove the peaceful population before
you like cattle into slavery; you separated
man and wife and forced them to hard
labor in trenches. I have seen the most
fiendish rape committed on young women,
and those who were forced into maternity
were cursing the father of their offspring,
and I began to doubt if my own inferno
was really up to date.

You have taken millions of dollars from
innocent victims and called it indemnity;
you have lived fat on the land you usurped
and sent the real owners away to starvation. You have strayed away from all le-
galized war methods and introduced a code
of your own. You have killed and robbed
the people of friendly nations and destroyed their property. You are a liar, a hyp-
ocrite and a bluffer of the highest magni-
tude. You are a pupil of mine and yet
you pose as a personal friend of God. Ah,
Wilhelm, you are a wonder. You wan-
tonly destroy all things in your path and
leave nothing for coming generations.

I was amazed when I saw you form a

partnership with the impossible Turk, the chronic killer of Christians, and you a devout worshipper in the Lutheran church. I confess, Wilhelm, you are a puzzle at times. A Mohammedan army commanded by Prussian officers assisting one another to massacre Christians is a new line of warfare. When a Prussian officer can witness a nude woman who is about to become a mother being disemboweled by a swarthy Turk, committing double murder with one cut of his sabre, and calmly stand by and see a house full of innocent Armenians locked up, the house saturated with oil and fired, then my teachings did not stop with you *but have been extended to the whole German nation.* I confess my satanic soul grew sick and there and then I knew the pupil had become the master. I am a back number, and my dear Wilhelm, I abdicate in your favor. The great key of hell will be turned over to you. The gavel that has struck the doom of damned souls since time began is yours. I am satisfied with what I have done; that my abdication in your favor *is for the very best interest of hell*—in the future I am at your Majesty's service.

Affectionately and sincerely,
LUCIFER H. SATAN.

"The devil taketh him up into an exceeding high mountain, and sheweth him all the kingdoms of the world, and the glory of them; and saith unto him, All these things will I give thee, if thou wilt fall down and worship me." Matt. 4:8, 9.

CHAPTER V.

THE PURPOSE OF THE KAISER.

There is no doubt but Satan has had the German Kaiser upon the high mountain of temptation, and has offered him world power. It is hardly likely that he appears to the Kaiser in his true character. It is quite probable that he manifests himself as the angel of German "kultur." He succeeded in making the Kaiser believe that he was the god of the universe when, in fact, he is only the god of this world; and under the delusion that he was the vicegerent of heaven to set up a better order of things on the earth. The deluded and devil-possessed Kaiser has proceeded to turn the earth into one vast slaughter pen.

There are no figures with which we can sum up and calculate the human suffering which the world has passed through during

the present great war.   It was not enough
that the Kaiser himself should be obsessed
with a diabolical passion to dictate world
affairs, but the people of Germany must be
so brought under his influence, and the
domination of the deluded and ensavaged
men who surrounded his throne, that they
would become the ready and willing agents
in the wreck and ruin of the nations of the
earth.

For the past seventy-five years destructive critics in the pulpits, colleges and universities, of the Central Empire, have prepared the German people for the merciless
slaughter of today.   A people to carry out
the orders of the Kaiser and his great gen-
erals, must be weaned away from the plain
teachings of the Holy Scriptures.   They
must imbibe the doctrines of evolution.
They must believe the race to be on its
way up, having just about arrived at
the ferocious stage of the tiger.
They must feel that irreverence for hu-

manity of which men will be easily capable when they conclude themselves and their fellow-beings to be a well developed breed of apes.

There is no doubt or question in our minds but the destructive critics of the great universities and pulpits of Germany have succeeded in making the German soldier what he is today—a furious, merciless, mad-man—the dread of all the earth, the heartless butcherer of unarmed men and helpless women, with their babes at their breasts.

From the very first, the German army has seemed to take a fiendish delight in destruction. They have turned beautiful cities into smouldering heaps of ruin and ashes, where no military advantage was to be gained. They have wasted tons of ammunition in the destruction of beautiful temples erected for the worship of God. They have outraged women, destroyed homes, broken up furniture, slaughtered dumb brutes, chopped down fruit trees, and if there is anything that they have left undone in the way of merciless destruction, that an army of fiends, out of the pits of perdition could accomplish, we fail to understand what it could have been.

Satan inspired the Kaiser with his ungovernable ambition. He rallied around him the blood-thirsty leaders of his cohorts. He saturated the German nation with skeptical teaching which destroyed the pure faith of Christian religion. He wrote question marks all over the Holy Scriptures; he brought them to deny and ridicule the inspiration of the sacred Book. They have questioned the Deity of Jesus Christ, and ridiculed the faith in Him which saves men from sin, and spreads abroad the spirit of fraternity and Christian fellowship. They have boasted that they would write a new Bible. Long before the Emperor drew his sword in this fearful world war, German destructive criticism had become the plague of the religious world. The unbelief fostered in their universities, was spreading abroad and doing great harm and hurt to the whole spirit of evangelical religion throughout the world. No country or denomination has escaped the baneful influence of the skeptical scholarship of the German universities.

Those arrogant teachers and preachers in this country who are following the lead of the destructive critics of Germany, are the most dangerous enemies of the Church, of society, and of this great republic. The men who destroy the faith of the people in the reliability and authority of the Word of God, do the people and the nation irreparable injury.

If Germany had been saturated with evangelical Bible truth, had the pure Gospel of a free and full salvation been faithfully preached throughout this nation, the present war, with its heartless cruelties, would have been a moral impossibility.

The religious and political literature of Germany reveals two great facts which account for present world conditions. One is, that the moulders of thought in Germany, with rare exceptions, have surrendered the faith in the inspiration of the Scriptures; and the other is, they have come to be devoted believers in war. They believe it is right to trample under foot the weaker nations of the earth; to go to any extent of the ruthless destruction of life and property in order to carry out their ideas of absolutism. Turning from Christ and His Gospel, they have come to worship ODIN, the god of war.

The number and character of the books on war, written by leading Germans within the last few years, is startling, and reveals the fact that the entire moral atmosphere of the nation was soaked and saturated with the spirit of militarism, and the erroneous and diabolical notion that "might makes right." In the light of all the facts at hand it cannot be doubted that the Kaiser and his coadjutors, while they have secretly planned and manufactured the great cannon of which the world knew nothing, the U-boat which they brought to an unsuspected perfection, and the Zeppelin, with its murderous bombs to rain upon the helpless people of undefended cities, and have had as the one end in view, *world power.* Undoubtedly, the devil has had the Kaiser up in an exceeding high mountain; and unconsciously, no doubt, the Kaiser has bowed the knee to his Satanic majesty. When he speaks of "Me und Gott," deceived in his own heart, he means "Me and Odin."

"For nation shall rise against nation, and kingdom against kingdom; and there shall be famines, and pestilences, and earthquakes, in divers places. All these are the beginning of sorrows." Matt. 24:7, 8.

CHAPTER VI.

THE HORRORS OF THE WAR.

The close of each dispensation has been signally marked by the judgments of God upon the wicked. The Scriptures clearly teach that the same will be true of the closing years of the present dispensation. God is merciful, slow to anger, and of great kindness, but He will not always chide, neither will He keep His anger for ever.

The nations have grievously sinned, and the time of God's judgments are upon us. Not Germany alone is guilty before God. The Sabbath desecration, the drunkenness, the unbelief, the blasphemy of the world are appalling. The vast multitudes of our population act as if there were no God; as if we had no revelation from Him, no laws to keep, no judgments to fear.

Take the sin of impurity alone, which

is the prolific mother of all vice and degradation.   In our allied nations in this great war we have so many base women, seeking the money, the vigor and health of our soldiers, that the government, struggling against the power of the Central empires, fear the lewd women of our own nations more than they do the armies of Germany. These are appalling statements, but they are sadly true.

All the world has sinned, and all the world must suffer; but Germany is the ambitious aggressor in this horrible war. She has set herself to overthrow civilization, to trample ruthlessly upon the liberties and rights of men.   She has disregarded the Holy Scriptures, and trained her guns against the very throne of God and righteousness.   The devastation and ruin she has spread through the earth, is without parallel.   It would be almost impossible to exaggerate the sufferings inflicted upon the Belgium people; the men who have been murdered, the little children who have perished because of hunger and exposure, the women who have been outraged, the families who have been broken up and shipped about in trains from one place to another like cattle, surpasses anything in all the records of human history.

This war, so long planned and prepared for by the ambitious Kaiser and his coadjutors, in which they have trained, officered, and armed the unspeakable and fiendish Turk, has led to the merciless slaughter of eight hundred thousand unarmed and helpless Armenian Christians. The thought staggers the mind. It is difficult to grasp the proportions of so horrible a tragedy. The Kaiser has done all in his power to inaugurate a religious war, turning the hordes of Mohammedans loose in merciless rapine to deluge the whole Christian world with fire and blood.

Palestine, which has been struggling to

her feet through the Zionist movement for the past century, in which many beautiful and thrifty colonies of returned Jews were beginning to bloom with some substantial prospect of peace and hope, has been ravaged and swept, as with a besom of destruction. Thousands of desolated Jews have fled for refuge down into Egypt, and others have perished from starvation and under the merciless sword.

The outrages perpetrated in that part of France, which has been invaded and held by the German army, cannot be described in human language. The suffering in Poland, especially among the Jews, is without parallel. Mr. Rohold, a highly educated and influential Jew, figures that not less than 500,000 Jews have perished in Poland and Russia as one of the fruits of this horrible war.

It is a scene too dark and awful to dwell upon. It is the outcome and fruitage of the insane ambition of a human being un-

der the deception and domination of Satan.
The Kaiser is not the final Man of Sin,
spoken of in the Scriptures, who shall almost entirely dominate and rule the world
in the closing days of this dispensation,
but he is the forerunner of this coming son
of Satan. He illustrates the possibility of
a human being swallowed up by ambition
to rule, and inspired and led on by the
spirit of all evil. There is no hope for
peace among men until his power is
broken, his followers, who rally about
his standards, are disillusioned, and Germany, herself, as well as the rest of the
world, delivered from the merciless grasp
of militarism.

No one human individual in all the world
has brought such suffering and ruin to all
the world, as the German Kaiser. In no
one instance has he instructed his soldiers
to spare a country or people; to show mercy to the unarmed and defenseless; to treat
with consideration the unfortunate mother

and infant who fell under the power of their savage and brutal grasp.

There is no language with which to describe the suffering which the insane ambitions of the German Kaiser and his war lords have inflicted upon the human race. There are no mathematics with which to calculate the number of soldiers slain, of citizens butchered in cold blood, of women outraged, of little children who have perished, of cities, villages, and homes laid in ashes, of churches destroyed, and the black crepe of sorrow hung upon the doorknob of hundreds and thousands of mourning homes. Language utterly fails to tell the fearful story of this world tragedy thrust upon the race by the proud and selfish ambition of a few men who have yielded themselves up as the deluded victims of the devil, who are described so graphically in the following words, found in Revelation, 12th chapter and 12th verse: "Woe to the inhabiters of the earth and of the sea! for the devil is come down unto you, having great wrath, because he knoweth that he hath but a short time."

In his hatred of God, of peace, and his furious desire to destroy the race and turn our earth into a smoldering heap of blood and ruin, Satan congratulates himself in having secured for his agent the Kaiser and his followers.

"The noise of a multitude in the mountains, like as of a great people; a tumultuous noise of the kingdoms of nations gathered together: The Lord of hosts mustereth the host of the battle. They come from a far country, from the end of heaven, even the Lord, and the weapons of his indignation, to destroy the whole land. Howl ye; for the day of the Lord is at hand; it shall come as a destruction from the Almighty." Isa. 13:4, 5, 6.

CHAPTER VII.

UNCLE SAM TO THE RESCUE.

No humane man can sit placidly on his front porch, reading his Bible, while a band of ruffians murders his neighbors across the street, outrages the women, maims the children, ransacks and burns the property. No prudent man could remain inactive under such circumstances, when he has positive proof that spies connected with this band of ruffians have already carefully inspected his premises, and marked his own home for the next in the order of destruction.

Germany had not only gone to war with a number of nations in Europe, but she had gone to war against the great fundamental principles of human freedom. She had begun a crusade against the entire spirit of democratic principles, and all re publican forms of government throughout

the earth. Her scheme of conquest knew
no boundary lines of nations, and spared
no people among civilized men from her
plan of rapine and murder, in her effort
for world mastery.

Germany not only sank the Lusitania in
violation of the laws which govern civilized people, but her entire diplomatic
corps, while professing friendship, were
acting spies and honeycombing the entire
nation with paid agents to prejudice and
produce disunion and strife among our
citizens; at the same time her hired incen-
diaries were setting the torch to our factories, and sending up millions of dollars
of valuable property in flames. Worse
still, her diplomatic corps was busy seeking to arrange to bring a vast Japanese
army into Mexico, and to turn the whole
Mexican horde of murderous, half-civilized
people loose upon our Western population,
with the promise of ample reward in the
gift of vast sections of our territory.

The ruthlessness with which Germany murdered our people, destroyed our property, and the hypocrisy with which she planned to thrust a cruel war upon us, with a full purpose of wresting from us vast regions of territory, is a species of diabolical hypocrisy unsurpassed in the diplomatic history of nations.

The patience and forbearance of the American nation, under the most powerful provocation, has never been equaled in all the conflicts of history. Hateful as war is, as much of suffering and sorrow as it involves, there was absolutely nothing left to the American people but to declare war against Germany. Germany had already, and had for some time, been at war against the United States. Not only had she taken many lives and destroyed millions of dollars worth of property, but was doing her utmost to turn against us a neighboring nation, and was ready to arm, equip, and officer the Mexican people to cut the throats of unarmed men, and outrage the women of the West, as the German army had done the women of Belgium and France.

The whole matter reduced itself to the simple proposition: Would the American people join the allied nations of Europe to fight against the Central powers, or would she sit supinely by while the Central powers crushed the civilization of Europe; meanwhile destroying our ammunition factories, sinking our ships, and her diplomatic corps sowing broadcast dissension and strife among our people, and in the end, our nation having to fight Germany alone, and unprepared, without the sympathy or assistance of any one.

There was but one thing left, and that was to meet Germany on her own ground, and fight for our existence. If a nation ever went to war on an honorable basis, and in a righteous cause, in this instance, it was our nation.   Our brave soldier boys are the advocates and evangels of human liberty. They are fighting for the rights of all men, the protection of the hearth-stones of the homes of all the world. They are giving up their lives that women and children may be saved from the horrible brutality of educated and scientific savages.

Whatever the sacrifice may be, the prize is worth the price. We cannot afford to see the wheels of progress turned backward, and the liberties and the hopes of men trampled ruthlessly beneath the feet of a merciless and conscienceless foe. This is humanity's war. Every American who loves his native land, his flag, his Bible, and his church, his grey-headed father, saintly mother, pure sister, sweetheart, and little children, has a part and parcel in this splendid sacrifice. Every one who can carry a gun to the battle front, swing a sledge at the forge, hold a plow handle, dig a trench, butcher a beef, drive a nail

or push a saw, offer a prayer or shed a
tear, may bear a part in this noble struggle of men who love God and the human
race, to free itself from a cruel and heartless militarism which knows no reason,
and respects no rights.

If there ever was a time when all political ambitions and prejudices should be
forgotten, when class distinction should
be obliterated, when denominational prejudice and bitterness should sink out of
sight, when rich and poor, capitalists and
labor, should all unite in the bond of sacred
brotherhood, stand up and stand together,
heart to heart, and shoulder to shoulder,
for a great good cause, that time is now.
The spirit that should characterize a nation is well expressed by Macauley in his
"Lays of Ancient Rome:"

> "Then none was for a party:
> Then all was for the State;
> Then the great man helped the poor,
> And the poor man loved the great."

In spite of the enemies who have striven
to sow dissension and strife among us, a
few cowardly and selfish politicians who
have feared the voting power, disloyal men
who enjoy the protection of our flag, and
the benefits of our civilization, and love a
foreign country; despite certain small bit-
ter-hearted newspapers and magazine pub-
lishers, who hate our President because
they cannot dictate his appointments and
policies, our nation has risen nobly to the
heroic task before her.

The farmer boy has left his plow in the
furrow; the university student has laid
down his scientific apparatus; the young
banker has quitted his desk; the lawyer
has left his briefs; the millionaire has forsaken his golf links and polo grounds; the
fisherman has thrown down his tackle;
many an idler has caught the spirit of the
movement, and hardened hoodlums have
risen to manhood, and come out of the
slums to take their places in the ranks in

the glorious army of freedom. Million-
aires have emptied their coffers, and homes
of scanty means have brought forth their
little savings to lay with glad hearts and
trembling hands, their willing sacrifice
upon the national altar.

A whole army of women have given
themselves nobly to the service of mankind. They are not only trained for
nurses, but they are ready to take their
places in the garden, the office, the factories, and anywhere, where a tender heart
and a strong hand is needed. Scores of
the wealthiest women of this nation have
forsaken their palaces and their pleasures,
and have gone into those regions most
ruined and ransacked by the war, to give
of their means and to succor the suffering.

The response of the American people to
the call of the Red Cross, with millions for
Y. M. C. A. work, and the supply of the
government, not only with means to pros-
ecute the war, but to assist the allied na-

tions, and to reach out a great hand of charity to the suffering multitudes, has been a marvel and delight, and is worthy of a great free people who have imbedded deep in their natures the principles of that honored American statesman, who, in a former crisis of our history, exclaimed, "Give me liberty, or give me death!"

Out of this sowing of wealth and heroic lives, human blood and tears, what shall the harvest be! We can but hope and pray that the Huns will be overthrown; we believe that victory will at last perch upon the banners of freedom. That, for at least a short period, peace may come back to our troubled world; that, out of the wreck and ruin of the war, the people may erect their homes and gather the fragments of broken families about their heartstone in prayer. But the German Kaiser and his war-mad slaves have inflicted a wound upon the human race which can never be healed; have committed a crime against mankind deep as the pits of doom, high as the dome of heaven, broad as the utmost confines of earth, and lasting as eternity.

.

"They have healed also the hurt of the daughter of my people slightly, saying, Peace, peace; when there is no peace." Jer. 6:14.

"For when they shall say Peace and safety; then sudden destruction cometh upon them." 1 Thess. 5:3.

CHAPTER VIII.

THE PACIFISTS.

The pacifist is the man who pleads for peace at any price. The burning of cities, the murdering of eight hundred thousand Armenian Christians, the ravishing of untold multitudes of women, the maiming and starving of children, does not disturb his equanimity. He can stand with an idiotic smile upon his countenance, while the victims of the Lusitania reach their helpless hands in vain for help from the ocean, and all Germany laughs at their agony. He says, "Peace, peace," while diplomatic representatives of a foreign enemy sow the seed of disintegration and internal strife, apply the torch to our factories, and offer Texas, New Mexico and Arizona as a tempting bait to a neighbor nation to make war on us.

All Christian men must be opposed to

war; and yet, intelligent Christian men must, some time, fight for the great underlying principles of righteousness, without which, Christian civilization would be impossible. The man who, from the standpoint of Christianity, objects to war, must have the sympathy and respect of his fellows, but he must not ignore the fact that we have wars thrust upon us, that the sacred shrines of Christianity are being destroyed, and the very foundations upon which we build every hope of human happiness here and hereafter, are being broken up, that the Bible itself is being attacked, the Deity of Jesus Christ denied, and the guns of the Huns trained upon the foundations of all religious truth.

The maudlin, fanatical pacifist reminds one of a strapping farmer, sitting upon the pasture fence, while a frightened woman is chased by a maddened bull, and instead of going to her help with a Winchester or pitchfork, calling to her to pac-

ify the animal by rubbing his nose with a
bunch of lilac blossoms. He is the kind of
man that would fall on his knees and beg
the policeman not shoot the poor mad-dog,
but teach the little children to tame the
docile, sweet creature by patting him on
the head, and feeding him with chicken
sandwiches.

These similes are not exaggerated.
There would be just as much solid and log-
ical reason in the methods of the pacifists
with the German war lords, as the proposed treatment of furious bulls and mad-
dogs. However tenderhearted and humane you may be, you have got for the
sake of society, to take pitchforks to the
bulls, and shot-guns to mad-dogs.

Most of the pacifists of this country who
claim to be opposed to war, are hypocrites
and liars. They do not believe in war,
and in the German method of war. They
wanted to escape military service in Germany and enjoy the privileges of this free

and democratic country, and now they
want Uncle Sam to stand quietly and hold
up his hands while they hold the U-boat,
the torch, and the mob of Mexico at his
head, pick his pockets of his liberties, and
sell his States to foreign invaders.
We have no enemies half so dangerous,
and who hate us with so deep and bitter
a hatred, as those political demagogues,
newspaper copperheads, and disguised
spies, who would rejoice to see our trans-
ports go down at sea, and our armies cut
to pieces on the French frontier. They
are busy seeking to bind the hands of the
administration at Washington; to prevent
our brave men from enlisting to defend
the honor of the flag. They would sink
the ships that carry food to the suffering
women and children in Belgium. They
would deposit explosives in great passen-
·ger vessels and send them down in mid-
ocean with all on board, without any com-
punction of conscience. They endorse and

gloat over the brutality and outrages of the German Kaiser. Like the unfortunate Jews who cried out on the sad hill of Calvary, "His blood be on us and on our children," they are willing and glad to share their part of responsibility for this horrible crime of the ages.

While the whole world longs for peace, and fights on with a hope that this may, at least, be the last war for a generation, German militarism is busy learning lessons from the present war, and planning preparations for the next. We clip the following from the daily press:

"An insight into the war-sodden minds of Prussian militarists is given by a book just published in Germany called 'Deductions From the World War,' a copy of which was received here today from Berlin.

"It is written by Lieut. Gen. Baron Von Freytag-Loringhoven, who was quartermaster general of the German army when Gen. Von Falkenayn was chief of the German general staff. Gen. Von Freytag is now stationed in Berlin as deputy chief of the general staff. His book breathes blood-and-thunder preparedness.

"After arguing that the German army must be expanded after the present conflict is over, Von Freytag continues:

"We shall have to continue to pursue this road in the future quite apart from the necessary increase in garrison artillery and technical troops. Moreover, when the number of those who have fought in the great war has fallen away, we shall have to aim at subjecting at least to a cursory training the men of military age who are at first rejected but who, in the course of war, have turned out to be fit for service, so that when war breaks out they may form a generous source of reserves.

"Only so can we arrive at a real people's

army, in which every one has gone through the school of the standing army.

"In the future, as in the past, the German people will have to seek firm cohesion in its glorious army and in its be-laurelled young fleet. Our business is to maintain the fundamental ideas of war as they lived in the German army up to 1914, to soak them in the experiences of the present war and to make the fullest technical use of them. But we must do all this without giving an entirely new direction to our thinking on strategy and tactics."

The last chapter of the book is called "Still Ready for War," and argues that Germany must be ready to plunge into fresh conflict after the present whirlwind of bloodshed and horror is over. Von Freytag expresses the opinion that as a result of Germany's position in Europe and in world politics, "German soldiers must reject all ideas of pacifism and internationalism."

The book goes on to say, after the war is over the sports of the boys of Germany must be arranged and utilized so as to put into them the spirit and training that will fit them for military service.

William Allen White, a well known and perfectly reliable correspondent, now with the armies on the front, tells of several instances where German officers, after being captured, and while being treated for their wounds, have tried to assassinate the surgeons of the Allies who were ministering to them. Their purpose was to thin out the doctors so the wounded in the hospitals of the Allies would not have proper attention.

It is a well known fact that, for some time, the German airships have been seeking out, and dropping shells upon hospitals, murdering the wounded and their nurses, trying to so disorganize and break up the Red Cross work that the wounded would die for lack of attention.

These are the wild human bulls and mad-dogs with whom the pacifists would make peace, and grant opportunity to make larger preparation for world slaughter on a more fearful and shocking scale. The promoters of peace under present conditions are the advocates of another, and if possible, a more fearful war. There can be no hope for any lasting peace until the spirit of militarism is entirely broken in Germany; and much as this is to be desired, the sad probabilities are that this deeply imbedded faith in war, as a means to national greatness, planted so deeply in the German mind, cannot be uprooted. However this war may end, the spirit of militarism will still live in Germany, and in the future as in the past, will secretly plan the destruction of civil liberties, and the conquest of the world.

"And I will cut off the chariots from Ephraim, and the horse from Jerusalem, and the battle bow shall be cut off: and He shall speak peace unto the heathen: and His dominion shall be from sea to sea, and from the rivers even to the ends of the earth." Zech. 9:10.

CHAPTER IX.

WHEN THE WAR IS OVER—WHAT?

World conditions at the present time present a sad and mixed problem for our contemplation. Out of this maelstrom of fire and blood we hope for peace, but those of us who read and believe the prophecies contained in the Holy Scriptures cannot hope for long, protracted peace, until the inauguration of a new dispensation.

There is one thing of which we may be perfectly sure: the ravages of war will not regenerate the race. Going into this war sinners, we shall not come out saints. When the last gun has been fired in this cruel conflict, the world will still be left with many vexing problems, and the human heart will remain rebellious and wicked. Selfish interests will form its combinations of capital, and labor will defiantly demand its price. Socialism, much of it illogical and unreasoning, will have made tremendous strides. The rich will continue to lock the precious products of earth in cold storage, and the poor will go fainting and hungry. Perhaps, not so openly, but in secret places, inventive genius will concentrate its stimulated powers for the discovery of destructive agencies, and behind closed doors, cabinets will plan measures for defensive and offensive war.

It is not at all improbable but that the United States may come forth from this conflict with less of the true democracy, and far more of the spirit of militarism than she possessed when she armed herself to go forth and fight in order to "make the world safe for democracy."

You may be sure that for many years the politics of this country will be dominated by the soldiers who fight in this war. Those of us who remember the Civil War recall the fact that at its close, both North and South, the people were represented in

legislative and congressional halls by the
old soldiers. It was almost a waste of
time for the man who remained at home
to become a candidate against a man who
could wave an empty sleeve, and tell of
heroic deeds on battlefield. The ex-soldier
got the vote. In this particular, history
will repeat itself; and for many decades
to come the policies of this nation will be
directed by the brave men who have led
their charging hosts over the top along the
Western front in France.

We have seen in a former chapter, that
German military leaders are already planning for the intensive training of the
rising generation of German youth for
military service. The rest of the world
will argue, whatever the conditions of the
treatise of peace may be, that if one great
representative nation prepares itself for
war, the other nations will be compelled
to do the same; and the strong probabilities are that in spite of the fearful lesson

of waste of property and loss of life in the present carnage, that all the great powers now at war will, after peace is declared, inaugurate a system of universal service; and it is quite probable that this great democratic country will be dotted over with vast army camps, and a heavy burden of taxes laid upon the people, to teach the millions of youths the use of arms.

Those statesmen who are telling us that this is the world's last great war, and that we shall have universal peace among men, are entirely out of harmony with the teachings of the prophetical books of the Holy Scriptures, the words of Christ, and the writings of the apostles.

We regret to write down here what our fellow-men will regard as a pessimistic view of the future; but we believe the Bible, and are compelled to be true to the great facts plainly foretold in its inspired pages. We are hoping for, at least, a short period of peace, following the close of this world war, for a time of great evangelistic and missionary movement. It is to be hoped that the chastened world will give the true ministers of grace an opportunity for the rapid spread of the Gospel: and that during the breathing spell, while deceived and selfish world-leaders prepare for the last tremendous struggle before the coming of Christ and His Kingdom, the Church will arouse herself to the long neglected task of preaching the Gospel in all nations, and to every creature.

If the Kaiser could have realized his dreams, if he could have crushed France within a few weeks after the opening of hostilities, if he could have wheeled upon Russia, broken and conquered her, if he could then have brought England to her knees, thrown his armies into Canada, and marched upon the United States, all unprepared to protect themselves, our great Eastern cities, with their factories of arms and ammunition could have been easily captured, Mexico would have been aroused against us, and Uncle Sam would have had to accept the Kaiser's terms of peace. With the immense indemnities he would have exacted, and the combined fleets of the conquered countries under his command, the Oriental people would have been helpless, and the German Kaiser would have easily been a world victor. But he is bound to fail; his dream can never be realized. History is in the "toe age" of Nebuchadnezzar's great image. The time of world empire has passed forever, until Christ shall come to reign. True, Satan's last effort in this direction will meet a large degree of success during that short period of domination of the Man of Sin, through whom, for a little while, he will more nearly approximate his plan of world dominion, than he has been able to do through the agency of Alexander, Caesar, Napoleon, or the bloody Kaiser.

The hand of prophecy on the dial plate

of the ages points to perilous times. We are approaching the close of the dispensation, and it will be marked by the outpouring of the vials of wrath upon a wicked and rebellious race which has trampled upon the commandments of God, plainly written in His Word, and rejected His mercies graciously offered upon the Cross. This is God's world; He created it, He owns it, He intends to rule it. He has absolute right on this globe, and He does not intend that it shall constantly be the arena of strife; that selfishness and sin shall butcher and starve and destroy the creatures made in His image, and redeemed by the sacrifice of His Son. He intends to inaugurate a new dispensation; to set up His Kingdom among men; to put the world under the control of the Prince of Peace; to cast out the devil who shall deceive the nations no more, and happy men, in brotherly love, will no longer sweat in the furnaces of fire, manufacturing the implements of war, but with songs of gladness they will beat their swords into plowshares, and bend their bayonets into pruninghooks.

"And in the days of these kings shall the God of heaven set up a kingdom, which shall never be destroyed: and the kingdom shall not be left to other people, but it shall break in pieces and consume all these kingdoms, and it shall stand forever." Dan. 2:44.

"And Jerusalem shall be trodden down of the Gentiles, until the times of the Gentiles be fulfilled. And there shall be signs in the sun, and in the moon, and in the stars; and upon the earth distress of nations, with perplexity; the sea and the waves roaring; Men's hearts failing them for fear, and for looking after those things which are coming upon the earth: for the powers of heaven shall be shaken. And then shall they see the Son of Man coming in a cloud with power and great glory. And when these things begin to come to pass, then look up, and lift up your heads; for your redemption draweth nigh." Luke 21:24, 25, 26, 27, 28.

CHAPTER X.

THE COMING KINGDOM.

When Christ was in the world He taught all His disciples to pray, "Thy Kingdom come; Thy will be done on earth as it is in heaven." This united prayer of all the members of His true Church through the centuries, unconsciously of course, by many of His people, has been, and is, for the Coming of Christ, the casting out of Satan, and the setting up of the Kingdom of God on earth, in which men shall live and walk in beautiful harmony with His will. A golden age in which the world shall be free from war, from the liquor traffic, from white slavery, from pestilence and famine; when the seasons shall be regulated into perfect harmony, the earth shall bring forth in abundance, and the desert shall blossom like the rose.

It is a common remark of those who do not understand the Divine program, that

the Millennium, because of the conditions
of war and strife, seems to be a long way
off. Such people have the false and un-
scriptural notion that the Millennium will
be gradually ushered in by the wisdom of
wise and generous world rulers; by
treaties of cabinets, the acts of congress;
by social service for the uplift of society;
by the building of schoolhouses, parks, and
playgrounds; by scientific sewerage system, and the introduction of the laws of
hygiene into the lives of the people; by
the passage of resolutions of religious con-
ferences and convocations; by the sat-
urating of the entire social life of the
world with the spirit of the Gospel.

This may be a fascinating dream, and
pleasing program, gotten up by men, but
it is entirely out of harmony with the
Scriptures. No nation has ever attained
a more advanced position in education, and
the development of all the branches of
modern science than Germany, but the

"kultur" of her mind has not sanctified her heart. Pride and ambition go hand in hand with human progress in the arts and sciences. Men are puffed up with their attainments of wealth and what they call knowledge, and drift away from the teachings and spirit of the meek and lowly Christ.

The wisdom of this world will never inaugurate a universal reign of peace and happiness. The Apostle Paul tells us that, "In the last days perilous times shall come. For men shall be lovers of their own selves, covetous, boasters, proud, blasphemers, disobedient to parents, unthankful, unholy, without natural affection, trucebreakers, false accusers, incontinent, fierce, despisers of those that are good, traitors, heady, highminded, lovers of pleasure more than lovers of God; having a form of godliness but denying the power thereof." These are to be the conditions of the closing days of this dispensation.

Every word of this prophecy of the inspired Apostle is fulfilled before our eyes in a marked and striking degree. The teaching of Paul is in perfect harmony, and corroborated by our Lord Jesus Christ's description of last-day conditions. Speaking of the end of the age, He says, "And upon the earth distress of nations, with perplexity; the sea and the waves roaring; men's hearts failing them for fear, and looking after those things which are coming on the earth." These teachings describe with absolute accuracy, present-day conditions. Jesus does not tell us that such conditions indicate that the Millennium is a long way off, but he says, "When you see these things come to pass, then look up and lift up your heads; for your redemption draweth nigh." It is in the very midst of these things, while the earth is full of confusion and war, distress and perplexity, that Christ says, "Then shall they see the Son of Man coming in a cloud with power and great glory."

As might be supposed, we have in the Scriptures a remarkable combination of prophecies concentrated about the tremendous events connected with the great change that shall come to our planet, with the close of a dispensation, the overthrow and casting out of the devil, the breaking up of the kingdoms of this world, and the inauguration of the Kingdom of God on the earth. The breaking up of world kingdoms has begun in a remarkable degree. The king of Belgium has been driven from his throne. Peter of Servia, has been driven from his country. The Czar of Russia is a prisoner in Siberia. King Alfonzo is trembling on the throne in Spain. The spirit of social democracy threatens the existence of the Hohenzolleren family in Germany. The King of Greece has fled from his capital. Confusion reigns throughout the earth. The stone cut out without hands is smiting the image of world power upon its feet, and it will break and grind to powder rapidly during the coming year.

The "times of the Gentiles" are almost ended. There is reason to believe that the British army will still drive "the unspeakable Turk" from Palestine, and the Hebrew people will come flocking back to Zion like doves to their windows. Events are moving at the double quick. Time no longer drags; it gallops. Those who watch prophecies and the daily papers, will be impressed with the remarkable fulfillment of the predictions of God's inspired seers.

It is high time that the Church, the Bride of the Lamb, made herself ready to be caught away from the "great tribulation" which shall break directly with a storm equal in its fury to Noah's flood, and the merciless horrors with which the Roman legions besieged and burned the Holy City. Let those who love the Lord see to it that their garments are made white through the power of His cleansing blood.

CHAPTER XI.

THE RESTORATION OF ISRAEL.

The recent capture of Jerusalem by a British army is the opening of a new chapter in the history of the Hebrew people, and is preparing the way for the restoration of Israel to the Holy Land.

The Scriptures are not more specific and positive on any subject than that of the restoration of the Jews to Palestine. We call the attention of the reader to the following passages of Scripture which refer to this restoration: "And it shall come to pass in that day, that the Lord shall set His hand again the second time to recover the remnant of His people, which shall be left, from Assyria, and from Egypt, and from Pathros, and from Cush, and from Elam, and from the islands of the sea. And He shall set up an ensign for the nations, and shall assemble the outcasts of Israel, and gather together the dispersed of Judah from the four corners of the earth." Isa. 11:11, 12.

We are not able to understand how careful Bible readers have overlooked prophecies like the above, and have failed to see that it is the Divine program to restore the Hebrews to Palestine. We quote the following from Jeremiah 23:7, 8: "Therefore, behold, the days come, saith the Lord, that they shall no more say, The Lord liveth, which brought up the children of Israel out of the land of Egypt: But, the Lord liveth, which brought up and which led the seed of the house of Israel out of the north country, and from all countries whither I had driven them, and they shall dwell in their own land."

We have recently seen in a secular paper from the pen of a brilliant writer who knows little or nothing of the Holy Scriptures, a very attractively written article in which he ridicules the idea of the restoration of the Jews. But we fully believe ·that Isaiah and Jeremiah were inspired, and that they wrote under Divine direction, and what they wrote will certainly come to pass. Not only do the prophets teach that Israel is to be restored, but there are many references in the writings of the ancient seers pointing to a great spiritual awakening and blessing upon restored Israel. Take, for instance, the following from Ezekiel: "Therefore say, Thus saith the Lord God; Although I have cast them far off among the heathen, and although I have scattered them among the countries, yet I will be to them a little sanctuary in the countries where they shall come. Therefore, say, Thus saith the Lord God; I will even gather you from the people, and assemble you out of the countries where ye have been scattered, and I will give you the land of Israel. And they shall come thither, and they shall take away all the detestable things thereof and all the abominations thereof from thence. And I will give them one heart, and I will put a new spirit within you; and I will take the stony heart out of their flesh, and will give them an heart of flesh: That they may walk in my statutes, and keep mine ordinances, and do them: and they shall be my people, and I will be their God." 11:16-20.

There is a class of Bible students who fail to see in these prophecies a promise of the restoration of Israel, and they are fond of calling attention to the barren and waste state of the land which has been brought about under Turkish rule through the long weary years of Israel's wanderings. But there are a number of promises in the Holy Scriptures that the blessing of God shall rest upon the land and bring about its restoration to fertility. Take, for example, Ezekiel 36:8-11: "But ye, O mountains of Israel, ye shall shoot forth your branches, and yield your fruit to

my people Israel; for they are at hand to
come. For, behold, I am for you, and I
will turn unto you, and ye shall be tilled
and sown: And I will multiply men upon
you, all the house of Israel, even all of it:
and the city shall be inhabited, and the
wastes shall be builded; and I will multiply upon you man and beast; and they
shall increase and bring fruit: and I will
settle you after your old estates and will
do better unto you than at your beginnings: and ye shall know that I am the
Lord."

With reference to the spiritual awakening which is to take place among the
restored Israelites, the following Scriptures are very clear: "And I will sanctify
my great name, which was profaned
among the heathen, which ye have profaned
in the midst of them; and the heathen
shall know that I am the Lord, saith the
Lord God, when I shall be sanctified in
you before their eyes. For I will take you

from among the heathen, and gather you
out of all countries, and will bring you
into your own land. Then will I sprinkle
clean water upon you, and ye shall be
clean. From all your filthiness, and from
all your idols, will I cleanse you. A new
heart also will I give you, and a new spirit
will I put within you: and I will take
away the stony heart out of your flesh,
and I will give you an heart of flesh. And
1 will put my Spirit within you, and will
cause you to walk in my statutes, and ye
shall keep my judgments, and do them.
And ye shall dwell in the land that I gave
to your fathers; and ye shall be my people, and I will be your God. I will also
save you from all your uncleannesses: and
I will call for the corn, and will increase
it, and lay no famine upon you. And I
will multiply the fruit of the tree, and the
increase of the field, that ye shall receive
no more reproach of famine among the
heathen. Then shall ye remember your

own evil ways, and your doings that were not good, and shall loathe yourselves in your own sight for your iniquities and for your abominations." Ezek. 36:23-31. All this shows that Israel is not only to return to the Holy Land, but there shall be among the restored people a great turning to God, and the land shall become abundantly fruitful. We cannot refrain from giving one more quotation from this same chapter which promises that great blessing shall rest upon the land. "And the desolate land shall be tilled, whereas it lay desolate in the sight of all that passed by. And they shall say, This land that was desolate is become like the garden of Eden; and the waste and desolate and ruined cities are become fenced, and are inhabited. Then the heathen that are left round about you shall know that I the Lord build the ruined places, and plant that that was desolate: I the Lord hath spoken it, and I will do it." Ezek. 36:34, 35, 36.

We have here God's most emphatic pledge that Israel shall be restored, that her spiritual life shall be greatly revived, and that the land which is, under proper cultivation, one of the most fruitful countries on the globe, shall become as the garden of Eden in fruitfulness. At least, the traveler looking upon the land shall pronounce it as the garden of Eden.

We are fully convinced that the recent capture of Jerusalem means the end of Gentile rule. The reader will recall that saying of Christ in Luke 21:24: "And Jerusalem shall be trodden down of the Gentiles, until the times of the Gentiles be fulfilled." We are happy to believe that the times of the Gentiles has been fulfilled, and that we are now at the beginning of the long-looked-for restoration; and at the close of the present war the Israelitish people, in large numbers, will return to Palestine.

Many of our readers are well acquainted with the "Zionist Movement," an organization of Jewish people who, for years, have been seeking the restoration of Israel, and, in fact, have brought back many Jews to Palestine. When the present war broke out Jerusalem was becoming a thriving city, and there were some forty prosperous Jewish colonies scattered over Palestine, many of them successfully engaged in agriculture. The war has practically put an end to this prosperity, and large numbers of the Jews have been driven back into Egypt, and not a few of them have joined the armies of the Allies.

Under the protection of Great Britain the Jews will come flocking home in large numbers, and directly the deserts of the Holy Land shall blossom like the rose. There is a class of Bible students who claim that during this war Jerusalem will again be captured by the Turks and Germans. We are confident they are mistaken. We believe that Jerusalem will re-

main under the protection of Great Britain
for several decades, giving ample time for
the development of the country and the
prosperous conditions indicated in the
Scriptures quoted above. In our eager-
ness to hasten the end of the dispensation
and see the inauguration of Christ for His
Millennial Reign, we must not ignore
prophecy which must be fulfilled before
our Lord appears.

CHAPTER XII.

THE BATTLE OF ARMAGEDDON.

That Jerusalem is once more to fall into the hands of the enemy is clearly taught in Zechariah 14th chapter, first and second verses: "Behold, the day of the Lord cometh, and thy spoil shall be divided in the midst of thee. For I will gather all nations against Jerusalem to battle; and the city shall be taken, and the houses rifled, and the women ravished; and half of the city shall go forth into captivity, and the residue of the people shall not be cut off from the city."

Some students of prophecy seem to think that this re-capturing of Jerusalem will take place during the present war. We believe they are mistaken, for the simple reason that this gathering of the nations against Jerusalem will evidently occur after the restoration, development, and enrichment of Israel; for other verses in the 14th chapter of Zechariah indicate that this fighting against Jerusalem shall take place immediately before the appearing of the Lord upon the Mount of Olives, and the great earthquake, which "shall cleave in the midst of the Mount of Olives toward the east and toward the west, there shall be a very great valley; and half of the mountain shall be removed toward the north, and half toward the south."

It seems quite impossible to us that these great events should take place before the present war closes; because that gives no time for the fulfillment of those prophecies quoted in a previous chapter, which promise the restoration, a spiritual revival, and the great prosperity of the restored Israelites.

Ezekiel, in the 38th chapter of his prophecy, evidently speaks of the same war against Jerusalem which is spoken of in the 14th chapter, first and second verses of Zechariah. Ezekiel's prophecy very clearly refers to something that will take place after the restoration and blessing of Israel. Let us begin with the eighth verse: "After many days thou shalt be visited: in the latter years thou shalt come into the land that is brought back from the sword, and is gathered out of many people, against the mountains of Israel, which have been always waste: but it is brought forth out of the nations, and they shall dwell safely all of them. Thou shalt ascend and come like a storm, thou shalt be like a cloud to cover the land, thou, and all thy bands, and many people with thee. Thus saith the Lord God; it shall also come to pass, that the same time shall things come into thy mind, and thou shalt think an evil thought: and thou shalt say, I will go up to the land of unwalled villages; I will go to them that are at rest, that dwell safely, all of them dwelling without walls, and having neither bars

nor gates, to take a spoil, and to take a
prey; to turn thine hand upon the desolate places that are now inhabited, and
upon the people that are gathered out of
the nations, which have gotten cattle and
goods, that dwell in the midst of the land."
This Scripture clearly indicates that after the Israelites have been brought back
and have become prosperous, their enemies
—perhaps Turks, Arabs, possibly Russ-
ians—and various peoples, seeing the
prosperity and unprotected condition of
Israel, will determine to make war against
Palestine and recapture Jerusalem. Palestine will no doubt be under the protection of Great Britain at the time, and
when this aggregation of enemies come up
to overrun Palestine, capture Jerusalem,
and destroy the Jews, Great Britain will
come to their defense and protection.
Take the 13th verse of the chapter from
which we are quoting: It seems to be the
answer of the British Lion to these ene-

mies of the Jews: "Sheba, and Dedan,
and the merchants of Tarshish, with all
the young lions thereof, shall say unto
thee, Art thou come to take a spoil? Hast
thou gathered thy company to take a prey?
To carry away silver and gold, to take
away cattle and goods, to take a great
spoil?"

It is seen at once that this quotation is
not the answer of Israel to her enemies,
but some one apart from Israel; undoubtedly the British, possibly, the whole Eng-
lish-speaking world. Now read from this
same chapter, beginning with the 14th
verse, to the conclusion of the chapter, and
you will see that God will mightily destroy
the enemies of Israel, just as Zechariah
teaches that the enemies gathered out of
all nations against Jerusalem shall be overthrown. The prophecy of Joel is in perfect harmony with the prophecy of Ezekiel
and Zechariah on the subject under discussion. They all three foretell the restora-

tion of Israel, her prosperity in Palestine, and the coming of a mighty host of enemies against them, and of the wholesale destruction of these enemies of Israel. Joel must have written several hundred years before Ezekiel, and perhaps, three or four hundred years before Zechariah; and yet, the three prophets all foretell the same events, frequently using almost identical language. We suggest that the reader note the striking similarity between the 38th and 39th chapters of Ezekiel, the 14th chapter of Zechariah, and the 3rd chapter of Joel.

The facts which we wish to fix in the mind of our reader is that it is not probable that Jerusalem will now be re-captured by the Turks. If it should be, this recapturing of Jerusalem is not the great battle spoken of by Ezekiel and Zechariah. If the Turks should recapture Jerusalem during this war we shall be greatly surprised, and feel quite certain that before

the war is ended they will be expelled, and
that the final treaty at the close of the
great world conflict will see Jerusalem and
Palestine fully restored to Israel, and pro-
tected by Great Britain and her allies,
immediately followed by a rapid emigra-
tion of Hebrew people from the various
countries where they have suffered oppres-
sion, to Palestine. If, for some reason, at
the close of the present war there should
be a treaty among the nations involved
that, for a time, hinders the return of the
Jews to Palestine, this delay must be of
very short duration.

The restoration to Palestine will be followed by a very general religious awakening. We are not prepared to say that it
will be a purely Christian revival; that the
Jews will, in a wholesale way, accept the
Lord Jesus as the world's Redeemer. The
revival may largely be an awakening
among the Jewish people in their ancient
beliefs, and a zeal for God, and a strict re-

turn to the teachings, forms, and ceremonies of the Old Testament Scriptures. This will be attended by a period of great development and prosperity. It is not to be supposed that the Jews of the United States and the British Isles will return to Palestine, although, doubtless, many of them will do so; but they will come in vast numbers from those countries where they have been oppressed and impoverished; and the wealthy Jews of the United States and England will pour millions of money into the great enterprise of bringing these oppressed people to the Holy Land, and establishing them therein.

We are living in one of the most remarkable periods of all history, when the prophecies which were uttered and written long before the birth of the world's Redeemer, are being fulfilled before our eyes; and the most convincing and indisputable proofs are being furnished that the Bible is an inspired Book; that the

holy men who wrote the prophecies were
inspired by Almighty God; and that we
may rest our faith, without hesitation or
fear, upon the firm foundation of Holy
Writ; being fully assured that God's
Word cannot fail or pass away, and that
the predictions written therein by His
ancient seers must inevitably come to
pass.

It must be remembered that we are living in times when events transpire rapidly.
Only think how quickly San Francisco was
restored. When the present war closes
the great ships which have been trans-
porting millions of soldiers can be used in
bringing back Israel to their beloved land
from which they have been wanderers for
many long, weary centuries. Jerusalem
will be rapidly reconstructed, and the
whole land, with modern implements of
agriculture, will be improved; the valleys
will wave with golden grain, and the hill-
sides will be covered with vast orchards

and vineyards of olives, oranges, and grapes. The busy bees, as in the olden time, will gather the sweetest honey in the world from the vast flower beds which bloom spontaneously throughout the Land of Promise; and thus shall time move forward rapidly to the fulfillment of those remarkable words of the Apostle Paul in the 11th chapter of Romans: "For if the casting away of them be the reconciling of the world, what shall the receiving of them be, but life from the dead?   For if thou wert cut out of the olive tree which is wild by nature, and wert graffed contrary to nature into a good olive tree: how much more shall these, which be the natural branches be graffed into their own olive tree? For I would not, brethren, that ye should be ignorant of this mystery, lest ye should be wise in your own conceits; that blindness in part is happened to Israel, until the fulness of the Gentiles be come in. And so all Israel shall be saved; as it is

written, There shall come out of Zion the
Deliverer, and shall turn away ungodliness
from Jacob   O, the depth of the
riches both of the wisdom and knowledge
of God! How unsearchable are His judgments, and His ways past finding out!"

It would seem that when the great world
war closes and the Jews are restored to
Palestine, the Christian Church is under
highest obligation to do all in her power to
offer the Gospel of the Lord Jesus Christ
to the returned Jews; and as the restoration will be brought about by Christian
nations, it is reasonable to suppose that
these returned Jews would at least hear
them with respectful attention, while the
prophets and the Apostle Paul give us good
grounds to hope that many of them will
receive the Gospel with gladness, and be
saved by faith in Christ.

We can hardly expect the great spiritual ingrafting spoken of by Paul, before
the return of Christ at the end of the age;

but we may expect, if the proper evangelical effort is put forth, that many Jews will be converted after the restoration before the appearing of Christ in His glory. The great battle, the conclusive conflict of the age, called **Armageddon**, is evidently to take place when the Man of Sin commanding the evil forces of the earth, shall have reached the zenith of his power, and assembled his forces to make war upon the returned Jews and their defenders. It hardly seems possible that this event can take place in connection with the present world conflict. As we have already stated, Israel must be restored, Jerusalem rebuilt, and Palestine recovered from its present desolate state and become a fruitful and plenteous land. It is then that the prophecy contained in Ezekiel 38th and 39th chapters, 3rd chapter of Joel, and 14th chapter of Zechariah will be fulfilled. The great battle of Armageddon will be fought around Jerusalem, and God will avenge Himself upon the enemies of the Jews. Ezekiel describes this as the most fearful of all human conflicts, and says, "And they that dwell in the cities of Israel shall go forth, and shall set on fire and burn the weapons, both the shields and the bucklers, the bows and the arrows, the handstaves, and the spears, and they shall burn with fire séven years: so that they shall take no wood out of the field, nor cut down any out of the forest; for they shall burn the weapons with fire: and they shall spoil those that spoil them, and rob those that rob them, saith the Lord God."

Farther on in the same chapter, we are told, "And seven months shall the house of Israel be burying of them that they may cleanse the land." These scriptures give us some idea of what the battle of Armageddon will be, and the fearful destruction that will befall the armies of the Man of Sin, the opposers of God, Israel, and their defenders. This same great battle is described in Joel in the following words: "Proclaim ye this among the Gentiles; Prepare war, wake up the mighty men, let all the men of war draw near; let them come up. Beat your plowshares into swords, and your pruninghooks into spears: let the weak say, I am strong. Assemble yourselves and come, all ye heathen, and gather yourselves together round about: thither cause thy mighty ones to come down, O Lord. Let the heathen be wakened, and come up to the valley of Jehoshaphat: for there will I sit to judge all the heathen round about. Put ye in the sickle, for the harvest is ripe; come, get you down; for the press is full, the fats overflow; for their wickedness is great. Multitudes, multitudes in the valley of decision: for the day of the Lord is near in the valley of decision The sun and the moon shall be darkened, and the stars shall withdraw their shining. The Lord also shall roar out of Zion, and utter His voice from Jerusalem; and the heavens and the earth shall shake: but the Lord will be the hope of His people, and the strength of the children of Israel. So shall ye know that I am the Lord your God dwelling in Zion, my holy mountain: then shall Jerusalem be holy, and there shall no strangers pass through her any more."

This same great battle described by Ezekiel, Joel, and Zechariah, each one showing that the unbelieving and wicked nations shall come up against Jerusalem, and be conquered and overthrown with the most fearful slaughter, followed by the reign of Christ, and great peace and blessing, is also referred to in the book of Revelation, in which the inspired writer speaks of three unclean spirits like frogs going "forth unto the kings of the earth and of the whole world, to gather them to the battle of the great day of God Almighty." Rev. 16:14.

We should like to impress upon the mind

of the reader that in all of these Scriptures referring to this last great battle of the present dispensation, the Second Coming of Christ is mentioned. For instance, take the 15th verse of the chapter just quoted: "Behold, I come as a thief. Blessed is he that watcheth, and keepeth his garments, lest he walk naked, and they see his shame." These are the words of Christ Himself, and they connect His coming with this great battle round about Jerusalem.

The 16th verse of the same chapter refers to the spot where the battle is to be fought. "And he gathered them together in a place called in the Hebrew tongue Armageddon." In identifying the prophecy of Ezekiel with the Armageddon battle in the 16th of Revelation, the reader should know that each one of those prophecies in describing the fearful destruction that shall come upon the unbelieving nations, a great earthquake is mentioned. Ezekiel says: "Surely in that day there shall be a great shaking in the land of Israel; so that the fishes of the sea, and the fowls of the heaven, and the beasts of the field, and all creeping things that creep upon the earth, and all the men that are upon the face of the earth, shall shake at my presence, and the mountains shall be thrown down and the steep places shall fall, and every wall shall fall to the ground." Ezekiel also refers to the falling of great and destructive hailstones.

Now turn to Revelation 16:18, and read: "And there were voices, and thunders, and lightnings; there was a great earthquake, such as was not since men were upon the earth, so mighty an earthquake and so great." In the 21st verse of the same chapter, there is also the same reference as in Ezekiel to the falling of hailstones from heaven, perfectly identifying these two Scriptures, along with Joel and Zechariah, describing the battle of Armageddon, the world's last great conflict, the end of the age, and the appearing of the Lord Jesus.

These tremendous transactions cannot occur during the present war, but history will move forward rapidly in preparation tor their occurrence. The reader's attention is called to the fact that the Bride of Christ is to be caught away sometime before these awful days of tribulation; therefore, it behooves every one to have their wedding garments ready, and their lamps trimmed and burning; for we are undoubtedly living in the last times, prophecy is fulfilling rapidly, and in the light of the Holy Scriptures we have every reason to hope that very soon these predictions referring to the close of this dispensation will have been fulfilled, and our Lord, Who rode in humility into Jerusalem, to hang upon the Cross and die for the redemption of the race, will come back in clouds of glory to sit upon a throne of universal empire and reign in peace and righteousness over all mankind.